BARRY AUBIN

THE SCIENCE OF

Telepathy

AND HOW TELEPATHY WORKS

The Science of Telepathy
Copyright © 2023 by Barry Aubin

Tellwell Talent
www.tellwell.ca

ISBN
978-0-2288-9082-9 (Hardcover)
978-0-2288-9081-2 (Paperback)
978-0-2288-9083-6 (eBook)

Table of Contents

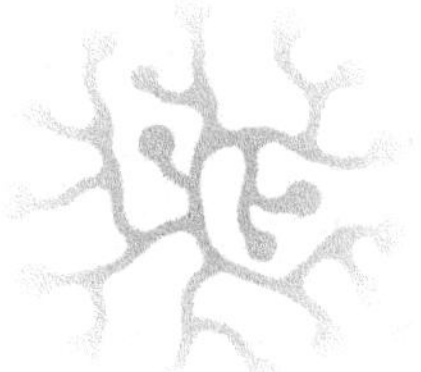

The Sixth Sense Introduction

THE USE OF TELEPATHY IS widespread but rarely discussed. I believe it is important to talk about the history of telepathy so that people know where it is going. The knowledge of telepathy and its use has been oppressed, and a mind-control dictatorship has existed for thousands of years. Because the Illuminati use mind control, the use of telepathy has been kept secret. Organized crime held government psychiatry to the assertion that talking about hearing voices is a sign of illness. This simply isn't true; however, during the mind control era, if someone talked about telepathy, their mind could get attacked, and they would end up mentally ill. It is no longer this way. I fought a war in the mind in which the crime group—a system-wide systemic oppression of people through mind control—simply died. While I write more extensively about the mind-control dictatorship in my memoir *My Life as a Telepathic Icon*, I will not go into it in detail here. It is important to know that the war of the Illuminati is over, but we can still get bad electrical signal attacks from space. However, we are in a new era where talking about telepathy will be more common rather than curtailed. Telepathy is as normal as hearing with our ears or seeing with our eyes. It is a sensory perception done by the brain.

This book aims to outline the facts and science about how telepathy works. It will be taught by the education system and policed by the judicial system. Few books that state the truth about telepathy exist, and since it is a new field, I will only use a few references in this book. Instead, I believe future books on this topic may reference me. I'm one of the first to write honestly on this topic. It simply wasn't safe in society to do so before.

I have been conscious of telepathy since 1999. This is not something that I made up to get sales. It exists, and I know because of a game I played with a neighbour. I asked him what time it was, and he told me the time telepathically from across the alleyway between our houses. Then, I checked the time on the clock, and my neighbour was right. We did this several times without fail. This proves that telepathy is real. I am not so clever as to make up the conversations that I have and have had using telepathy. It is not hard to notice the personalities co-existing in your head as you move from place to place, and when you see an aura—an electrical visual manifestation—you know you are seeing it and not hallucinating.

People have been telepathic for thousands of years. Our brains haven't evolved much since then. Most of the general population can be telepathic, and most of those who make up the remaining population are most likely kids who haven't learned yet. Telepathy wasn't discussed much in the past because people would be accused of witchcraft and hanged. It isn't talked about much today because it's easy to label someone as schizophrenic, bipolar, or psychotic and lock them up in a psych ward. Sure, it's harmless enough if it doesn't interfere with our everyday lives. But the stigma associated with telepathy being odd, weird, and socially unacceptable is real. That is why very few people (even scientists) know that telepathy has been proven in thousands of repeated experiments all over the world.

Another reason why telepathy is not mainstream is that its source cannot be guaranteed. For many, tracing the source of telepathy is almost impossible, making it awkward to discuss. I am writing about telepathy freely because I am unconcerned with the consequences of being labelled a social misfit. I also feel that a written discussion of telepathy stating the hard truth is far superior to homemade trial-and-error experiments, pranks, jokes, and flirtations with mental illness diagnoses.

I find it frustrating that when I look up telepathy and the sixth sense in reference books, I find them grouped with spirituality, near-death experiences, fictitious voodoo, tarot cards, astrology, sensing the future and past, communicating with the dead, and reincarnation. While learning about such things is one's choice, there should be a definite separation between what exists (the sixth sense) and what is experimental (tarot cards, astrology, voodoo dolls). Spirituality is a form of religion, and the two should be grouped together. The sixth sense should be defined as telepathy and auras, and it should be placed with language.

Despite the claims of some spiritual books, recognizing your sixth sense has nothing to do with eating the right foods, quitting smoking, and achieving an alkaline state. While being healthy is great and could benefit you spiritually, the sixth sense refers to opening yourself up to your subconscious mind. To do so, one must increase morality to learn the intellect required. I have found that many children can communicate telepathically, sometimes from birth. Some people, like me, weren't aware of telepathy until we were much older. While I am sure I heard other people's voices in my mind before the age of 22, I never made the connection with telepathy, attributing my thoughts to my vivid imagination. Some people never make the connection and live their entire lives in a non-telepathic way. This is fine, but not half as enjoyable.

I found discovering my telepathic self exciting. For a while, I couldn't believe it. My emotions progressed from awe at my newfound ability to anger for having missed out on such a wonderful thing for so long, and finally, to happiness that I could understand my own mind. It took three years for me to adapt to being telepathic. The process may have happened faster, but fame got in the way. When I finally woke up from my daze, I was world-famous; I was the Telepathic Icon. I can't say I was always on every channel and every radio station, but I listened to them telepathically and was always talked about.

The reason I became famous was not that I was unique. In fact, I discovered that many have the same gift. Nor was I witty or different from everybody else. My fame came because I "telepathized" everything I heard. In other words, every sound I heard, I turned into telepathy. Just imagine that when I drive by, you can hear the music I am listening to in your mind, even though my windows are rolled up. This is rather unusual. In fact, I am the only one on the planet who does this (or the loudest one). Over the last few years, I have not heard about anyone with the same ability. After a while, television anchors and radio DJs would telecast themselves onto me and ask me questions. By answering, I would become a part of their live telecast. For me, this meant not only adapting to telepathy but becoming a celebrity as well. I also had to adapt to being telepathic, and very few people on Earth were.

I was different from everyone else since birth. Others didn't notice this until first grade when I read lips to help myself hear the teacher. As a baby, I would writhe in agony, my hands covering my ears, whenever my parents put on the car radio. What caused my pain were high-pitched static sounds in my head. As soon as the radio was off, I was fine again. I could not communicate my discomfort to my parents, who did everything they could to help. They took me to numerous specialists who performed every test in the book, from cat scans to hearing and intelligence tests. Once, they hooked my head up to a bunch of wires and had me follow a bright light on the ceiling. The specialists found that my hearing and intelligence were above average and diagnosed me with hyperactive brain activity and an auditory processing deficit problem. This means that I could hear well but couldn't process sounds in the presence of background noise. Looking back, I think that the hyperactive brain activity was the cause of my telepathizing everything I heard. Of course, this was never expressed to me orally, only through telepathy.

The pain went away when I was about eight years old. I was pulled out of hockey for fear that I would injure my head. As a kid, this was difficult because I couldn't understand why I was so different. I had to take a pill called Dilantin, an anti-epileptic seizure drug, and I didn't like that either. It was then that my mother and I decided that I would go off my medication. I simply didn't want to be different from my peers. Today, after discovering my telepathic ability, I welcome these differences. I am still angry that my parents and doctors tried to take away my gift with pills that probably reduced my life expectancy.

Being a telepathic celebrity has its pros and cons. It's nice to be able to go places and have everyone know who you are, to have people remind you about what you need to do each day, to use your aura to shake hands with countless people and be telepathically announced when you enter a building. Because of my fame, I must strive to be a better role model. Since the media so publicized me, I am an open book and make instant friends everywhere I go. On the other hand, I must be careful about where I live since if I live on a busy street, people telecast into my house night and day, bothering me. Since I telepathize everything I hear, I also distract my neighbours when I watch TV and listen to the radio. I learned later in life how to shut off telepathizing everything I heard and to turn it on at will. I find it awkward to be famous and have no one go up to me and orally express his or her knowledge of my being a Telepathic Icon. In fact, all my social interactions are done through the sixth sense. Ironically, I am one of the most famous people in North America, yet I have not signed a single physical autograph. To date, a few strangers slipped and called me by my first name, and a few cashiers said, "Thanks, Mr. Aubin," even though I paid cash and never saw them before. But 99.9 % of the time, my status as a celebrity is entirely in my head.

While writing this book, I received a lot of telepathic threats from the Illuminati and Elders, stating I would be placed in a psych ward, but I didn't take it seriously. Being put in the psych ward for a month isn't the end of the world. In that case, I would have more time to write. However, my fame will ensure that it isn't long before my book on telepathy is announced in the media. When I told this to the Illuminati and Elders, some left me alone, while others threatened me telepathically with death. I didn't take their threats seriously (I have heard worse things before), but I realize that the Illuminati are adamant about keeping telepathy secret. That is why I needed to write this book quickly.

The Elders, who are afraid of the Illuminati, believe telepathy should not be discussed. They are adamant in their beliefs since they've only known this all their lives. The younger generation has an education that has an appreciation for science and is more open-minded to talking about telepathy. One of the reasons telepathy is kept secret is that people who are telepathically advanced tend to get better jobs. As a Telepathic Icon, I noticed that employers would run job advertisements through me while driving, sending subliminal messages to sell their products. Every employer I talked to uses telepathy and the sixth sense more readily than the blue-collar worker. Of course, you need strengths other than the sixths sense to succeed in business, but it is an important piece of the puzzle.

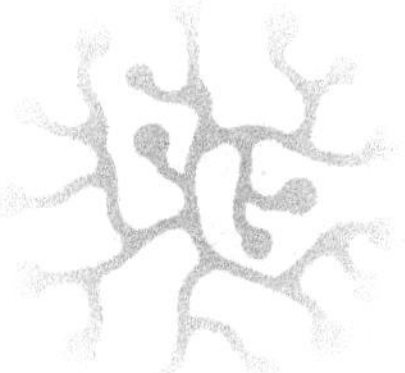

The Science of Telepathy

TELEPATHY ISN'T THAT COMPLICATED. IT is simply electrical signals your brain interprets from sources other than your brain. They sound like thoughts, but one must realize that thoughts are electrical signals that can come from anywhere in the universe. If we were ever to contact aliens, it would happen telepathically first. The day a person becomes telepathic is when they realize all the thoughts in their brain are not theirs. Of course, the government recognizes this as the day a person becomes mentally ill as they admit they hear voices, but is mental illness a choice then?

If you can hear your own thoughts, you can hear other people's thoughts. Everything comprised of electrons is telepathic. All electrons transmit electrical signals. Electrons are consciousness. All electrons can hear and receive electrical signals.

Electrons are everywhere. All electrons emit electrical signals. Am I mentally ill because I admit I hear electrical signals that aren't part of my brain generating the thought? Of course not. What happened is that the government was placed in a position where they had no choice but to make this wrong assertion because the telepathic crime dictatorship of the Illuminati had ganged up on them in telepathic crime mind control and forced them to act that way. In their minds, it isn't true, but at least if everyone keeps quiet about telepathy, they can't get in trouble with telepathic criminals. Zillions of Illuminati clones outnumber the people in government; thus, the people in government act in the only way they can. I clear the government of any wrongdoing in this regard, but once the zillions of Illuminati criminals are taken down, the government should act more honestly about the truth of electrical signals.

Vectoring: Vectoring is where evil such as organized crime, gang up on one person telepathically. It causes an effect of overpowering an individual through mind control. To defeat a vectored telepathic threat, one must have more vectored mass than the enemy to defeat it, which is why in a fight against zillions of clones and other combined evil groups, the vectored military person must be extremely famous to survive a telepathic attack and must be more numerous than the enemy.

We are not accused of mental illness when we admit that an electrical signal came down a wire from one computer to another, allowing us to read emails sent via electrical signals. Therefore, the brain should not be any different. However, plastic shields the electrical signals of a computer from leaving the wire so they can arrive at their destination from the source, but my brain is not encased in plastic and never will be. So, the scalp, hair, skin on our head, and skull all transmit electricity, meaning electrical signals can certainly enter the brain. If the volume of electrical signals is within a certain range, my brain will interpret them.

The spiritual realm is the same as telepathy or electrical signals. Telepathy is the means of communicating with electrical signals, and it all happens in the spiritual realm. The brain interprets electrical signals. And within the confines of the electrical signal, it is possible to represent electrical signals through the five senses—smell, taste, touch, sight, and hearing. So, we interpret electrical signals with our own five senses through our physical realm, but also in the spiritual realm. The five senses can be duplicated with an electrical signal. It happens all the time that the five senses are represented without the physical. A thought in the mind transmitted elsewhere in the format of the five senses happens frequently.

A person needs to be positively or neutrally charged to gain great intellect in general, including spirituality. This refers to the electrons that comprise a person's consciousness. Each electron of a person's soul or consciousness must not be negative. If you analyze what happens on an atomic level when an electron is negative, it is attracted to the proton of the atom's nucleus. Through electromagnetism, the negative is attracted to positive charges. This moves an electron closer to a proton, and the electronic field contracts. This contracted electronic field means the person will be less intelligent and have a lower speaking electronic frequency. When electronic fields are low energy and negative, they are cut off from the great intellect of the universe. This is like a safety mechanism built into the physics of the universe; if you are destructive, evil or negative, you will not have great knowledge. It is a choice to be neutral; when we are, the electrons move away from the protons. It's a choice to love the positive Earth, which expands your electronic field. Some people may not be able to learn about telepathy because their electronic field is too negative to gain the knowledge.

The electron is consciousness. I extensively write about it in the *Science of the Afterlife: Electron Consciousness Theory.* Quite simply, our minds, thoughts, and consciousness are electronic. Thoughts are electrical signals. Our nervous system transmits electrical signals. The electrons in our brain are our consciousness, and electrons are everywhere throughout the universe. Each electron is consciousness, and all electrons transmit electrical signals.

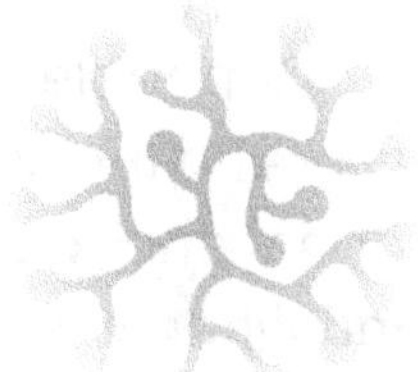

Telepathy Facts

THE MOST FAMOUS TELEPATHY EXPERIMENT was conducted during the Apollo 14 mission in 1971. NASA did not approve of this experiment. The astronaut, Edgar D. Mitchell, conducted the experiment on his own. To determine whether distance was a factor in telepathy, he read a series of 200 hundred numbers to four recipients on Earth. The mean for guessing the right number was 40, with two recipients getting 51 numbers right. While this doesn't necessarily substantiate as solid proof as some might claim, I believe that the proof lies in the fact that the astronaut believed in telepathy enough to carry out the experiment. "As astronaut Edgar Mitchell put it: "There are no unnatural or supernatural phenomena, only very large gaps in our knowledge of what is natural, particularly regarding relatively rare occurrences."

Telepathy has a long history. In 1885, telepathy was scientifically tested by the American Society for Psychical Research. The test placed a transmitter and a recipient in two different rooms. The transmitter broadcasted the recipient several visual images, a taste, and two-digit numbers. The scientists calculated mathematical probabilities following the experiment and concluded that telepathy existed.

Belief in thought transference in the year 2000 by the Ministry de la Recherche was that people who believed in thought transference was 40%, those who didn't was 58%, and those who had no comment was 2%.

I personally believe that the 58% who didn't believe in thought transference were part of the mind control group committing telepathic crimes. The problem with telepathic crime is that widespread and telepathic criminals hide the truth about the existence of telepathy.

All people are telepathic, but our ability to admit it is lacking. Organized crime is vast, and the use of mind control techniques and technology makes it incredibly difficult for anyone to speak or openly write about telepathy. A telepathic war is taking place, and when it is over, it will be easier. However, there may be increases in our abilities to communicate as time goes by as safety is increasingly achieved.

According to leading scientists, neural interfaces that link human brains to computers using artificial intelligence will allow people to read other people's thoughts. Facebook and Elon Musk's Neuralink are already developing brain-computer interfaces, and the report estimates that by 2040, neural interfaces will be an established option for effectively treating diseases like Alzheimer's. "People could become telepathic to some degree, able to converse not only without speaking but without words through access to each other's thoughts at a conceptual level. This could enable unprecedented collaboration with colleagues and deeper conversations with friends," the report says. "Not only thought but sensory experiences could be communicated from brain to brain. Someone on a holiday could beam a 'neural postcard' of what they are seeing, hearing, or tasting into a mind of a friend back home." Perhaps the writer of the article can only admit telepathy happens through electrical signals through technology and neuro interfaces but cannot admit the brain transmits electrical signals as well and doesn't need a neuro interface.

I did not learn about telepathy from my parents or teachers. I learned about it through the power of my own mind and observations within it. I was also taught by others telepathically. One of the biggest rules of telepathy is that you answer the sixth sense with the sixth sense and oral communication with oral communication. Mixing the two is breaking the rules and running the risk of being diagnosed with a mental illness or being committed. In fact, even if you talk about telepathy or try to read someone's mind on purpose, you are perceived as abnormal.

I often wonder why my parents didn't talk to me about telepathy. Perhaps this was because I was famous, and they didn't want me to become conceited. Perhaps they didn't talk to me about it orally and tried to teach me about the power of my mind by using theirs. After some time, they probably gave up since I couldn't hear their mental voices. It wasn't until I was in my twenties that I finally discussed it with my family. With my mother, I could only discuss telepathy in my mind. With my father, stepmother, and uncles, I could announce that I was telepathic. Their response was to ask how it felt to be world-famous. At the time, I didn't know how to respond to their questions because I hadn't fully realized the extent of my fame. Later, I talked to my father and stepmother in private, and they told me that they realized their telepathic ability at 32 and 16, respectively. Why they hadn't talked to me about it sooner was beyond me. Perhaps they were waiting for me to mature. A few years later, when I was at university, a fellow student I didn't know came up to me in the street, seized my head with his hands, and declared that telepathy existed. This is when I concluded that every person is different when it comes to the way they learn and communicate about telepathy. I have also decided that I will discuss telepathy with my kids orally at first and will teach them not to talk about it with strangers.

Telepathy does not involve constantly hearing a barrage of thoughts. For me, and I assume for others, it comes one voice at a time. In telepathy, instead of trying to read other people's thoughts, you say something in your head and wait for a reply; if you don't get an answer right away, it means nobody's listening, and you should try again later. One of the greatest challenges in learning telepathy is being able to sort the thoughts in your head as yours and others'. We all have a voice in our heads, which is our consciousness. You must only purposely say something in your head to hear your voice. Of course, we can change our mental voice to anything we want, but we tend to use the same voice naturally. After you've heard your voice, wait and listen. Anything that pops into your head spontaneously and does not sound like your voice probably isn't you. When you hear a voice that isn't yours, try to engage it in a conversation by saying something on the same topic. You will be surprised at the result. Then, practice and practice. It took me months and a lot of patience to master telepathy. Remember that those around you are probably used to not talking to you telepathically, and it might take a while to establish communication and develop a relationship. As you learn telepathy, remember that, at first, you are vulnerable. Be careful not to fall in love or become so infuriated with a voice that you search for its owner. The first rule of telepathy is that things in the sixth sense don't carry over into the world of oral communication. To keep a sense of normality, answer telepathy with telepathy and oral communication with oral communication. Keep things separate. Don't answer telepathic thoughts with verbal communication.

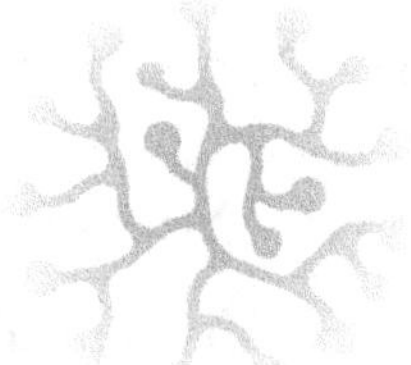

Baby Language

BABY LANGUAGE IS THE MAINSTAY of communication for many telepaths or beginner telepathy learners. The term "baby language" is not meant as a putdown. It's a nickname that reflects the fact that when you begin using telepathy, you pronounce every word one after the other. This is normal. In fact, this is how I still communicate to this day. It is a reference to down-low speaking. There are different frequencies in electrical signal communication. The most down-low frequency has been called baby language. If a person is an evildoer, such as breaking the Ten Commandments of Moses, they tend to have a negative electron composition to their consciousness. The negativity causes the electron to be attracted to the positive proton in the atom and causes the frequency to lower. Although a moral person can hear on all frequencies available to them, evil people will always have a limit and will never be able to hear the higher frequencies until they have made amends for their evil behaviour. They will also lose or not know the knowledge provided by higher electronic frequencies. This is a safety mechanism of the universe built into the physics that evil will never be able to dominate. Good will always be more able and smarter and can defeat evil. If a person wants to hear on higher electronic frequencies, then it is an absolute must that they learn morality, stick to it, and amend their conscience to attain this ability.

The Ten Commandments of Moses as provided by lifehopeandtruth.com:

1. You shall have no other gods before Me.
2. You shall not make idols.
3. You shall not take the name of the Lord your God in vain.
4. Remember the Sabbath day and keep it holy.
5. Honour your father and your mother.
6. You shall not murder.
7. You shall not commit adultery.
8. You shall not steal.
9. You shall not bear false witness against your neighbour.
10. You shall not covet.

From the Ten Commandments, I usually pay attention to not lying, stealing, murdering, and committing adultery. I also don't have any gods before the true creator of the universe. I have found that following these five and doing them in all aspects of life leads to enlightenment.

However, some clarification is needed on adultery. It isn't the simple act of sex that is sinful. If it were, procreation would be a sin, and the entire human race would die out. The creation of life is not sinful, but it depends on how you do it. If a person enters a sexual relationship, it must be of consent by both partners. The purpose of sex is to create life and bondage. If a child is born, it is a lifelong commitment to the spouse and child.

While it is easy not to steal, rape, or murder someone, not lying is the hardest of them all. In every moment of your life, the ability to lie is present. People can lie at almost every opportunity. To be truthful in every moment of your life is a challenge.

To not have any gods before the true creator of the universe is easy, but it is a personal relationship between you and God. When learning about telepathy, I had to be wary of people posing as God telepathically and pretending they were Him. So please learn to decipher mimics.

Honouring your mother and father is important, but it doesn't always mean doing everything they say. Sometimes it means doing the right thing even if your parents aren't. It means understanding what it means to "honour them." Doing the right thing all the time will do just that.

Not bearing false witness against your neighbour is important, and not coveting their house and spouse makes for good political peace-keeping.

Also, avoid anything that would make you feel guilty. I always think before I do things. I weigh the scenarios in my head, hear a voice, and know it is my conscience. I've found this faint voice is the voice of God. I listen to it always, no matter how hard things get.

I do not follow Christianity, but I go with much of the Old Testament, and I cannot find anything wrong with the Ten Commandments of Moses as a guide to becoming more neutrally charged in the electrons and being in a state of higher electronic frequency. Avoid negative choices and behaviours, and be positive!

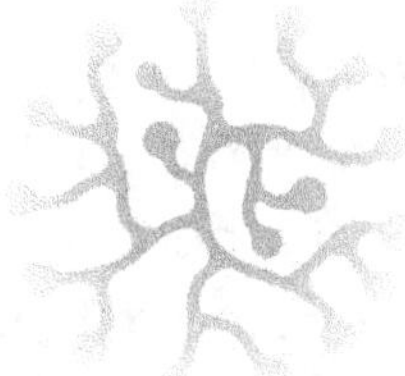

Speed Talking

FOR THE MORE ADVANCED TELEPATHY users, speed talking is a great option. The contents of communication are compressed: rather than saying a whole word or sentence, you only say whole paragraphs or other larger volumes at a time. This lessens the volume of communication. While I can speed talk, I don't tend to because quick communication may result in misinterpretations and misunderstandings. I can understand speed telepathy 90% of the time. It is frequently used in upscale neighbourhoods, corporate offices, white-collar working environments, and university campuses.

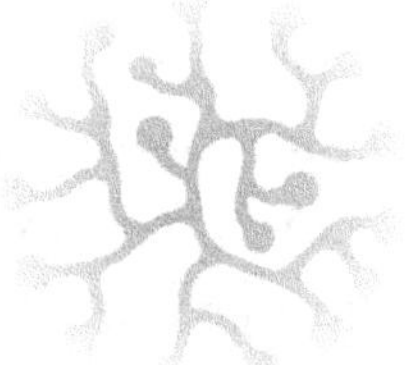

Double Speaking and Double Listening

DOUBLE SPEAKING IS A WORK of art. When I first heard it, I was amazed at the level of skill and intellect it involves. Double speaking means transmitting telepathic messages and expressing thoughts orally simultaneously. Sometimes the two conversations are entirely different. The ability to hold two different conversations at the same time is impressive. I am not very good at double speaking. Once, I was at a karaoke party, singing in front of several people. During my performance, a telepathic voice kept asking me questions. During pauses in my singing, I would reply to the voice, saying that I couldn't double speak. In a few seconds, I realized that I was, in fact, double speaking. It felt natural and easy at the time, but I have not been able to duplicate the experience since. I attribute this to the fact that I don't talk much. I sometimes practice by humming out loud while trying to express another thought in my head. However, I am usually not successful. My parents both use double speaking regularly. Most of the telepathic world can do it as well. I'm sure that it's a prerequisite for every TV and radio personality, but, of course, they would never admit to it in this world where telepathy is rarely talked about physically with verbal communication or written form.

I found double listening easier to master. Double listening involves listening to telepathic and oral communication at the same time. It was hard at first, and I would alternate between the two. However, listening to TV announcers and the radio while also listening to telepathic messages gave me a lot of practice. I sometimes felt that my sinuses were getting congested when I flipped back and forth between telepathy and orality. However, once I got some practice, double listening felt completely natural. Now, many years later, I feel I can have thousands of telepathic conversations simultaneously while communicating verbally on different topics.

As a person gets older, having two conversations telepathically at once can go into numbers much higher than two.

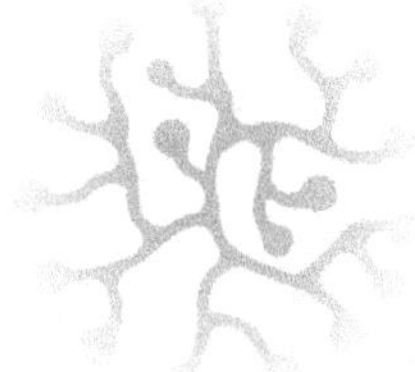

Directing Your Voice

MY FATHER ONCE TOLD ME that telepathic messages could be transmitted through the eyes. While I don't believe this is true, looking toward your target can certainly help. I have witnessed people transmit telepathic messages to people on their left, right, back, and front, all without moving their heads. While I have been able to do this on numerous occasions, I find it uncomfortable and prefer to turn my head in the direction I want to transmit.

Since my father and I awoke to our telepathic abilities late in life, we may have formed these habits by unconsciously talking forward all these years. Instead, you should pick a spot in your head and talk at it. While hearing from all directions requires no effort, talking in all directions is challenging for some and easy for others. We naturally talk forward, so answering a voice in your head that is coming from behind you without looking in that direction requires effort and conscious thinking. In time, however, it becomes natural.

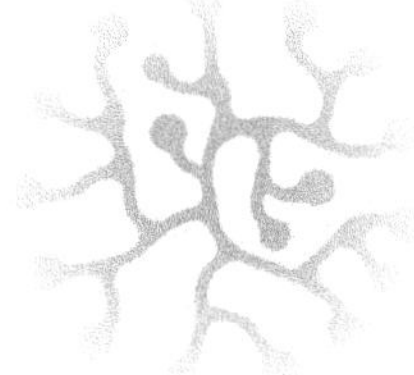

Hear Blocking

HEAR BLOCKING HAPPENS WHEN AN unknown force cuts off telepathic communication. Mothers often use hear blocking when they do not want their children to hear something, for example, a curse word. Hear blocking often happened to me when people wanted to say something behind my back. Frustrated, I pleaded for someone to show me how to do it. It was then explained to me that hear blocking could be as simple as putting aura hands over a person's ears. However, when I tested this method, it didn't work. Another person told me you must concentrate on auditory nerves to block hearing. I tried focusing on auditory nerves to generate interference, but it didn't work either. The answer finally came when I was driving. I was listening to a song on the radio when suddenly I heard a loud clicking noise in my head. This noise blocked out a swear word in the song. The person who communicated the noise told me to make that noise any time I wanted to block something from my hearing. I practiced this technique, and it worked amazingly well. Its premise is that you can override a telepathic noise with a louder telepathic noise. So, when you direct a loud telepathic noise at someone, that person cannot hear anything else for the duration of the noise.

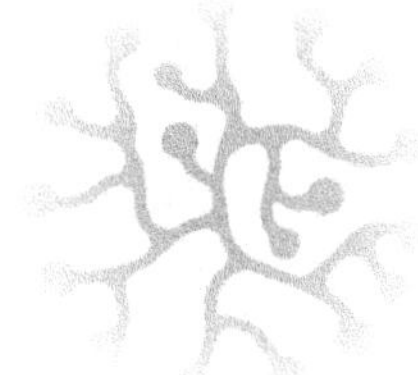

Telecasting

TELECASTING IS THE MOST ADVANCED form of telepathy, which involves projecting oneself long distances. A person miles away can hear you, communicate with you, and project their aura onto you. While I am still working on my telecasting skills, many of the telepathic community, mostly women, have mastered this skill. Some people have telecasted me across an entire city. In the beginning, I was concerned by such projections. I spend a lot of time in my car, where most of my telepathic communication happens. After awakening to telepathy, I arrived at a distance of about eight car-length as my transmission radius. Therefore, I was initially convinced that everyone communicating with me was within that distance. I would take frequent turns while driving to ensure people weren't following me. It was only later that I discovered telecasting and understood how it worked. The bigwigs and the upper middle class mostly use this gift. Men seem to do it less unless they have authority, and it seems to develop later in life for men. Almost all women seem to do it as they always seem to be bonded to their children and watch over them all day. Mothers often make a telepathic link with their husbands and children almost all day.

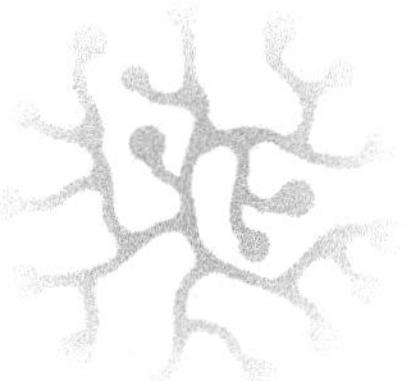

Telecast Seeing

ONE OF THE MOST IMPORTANT aspects of telecasting is the ability to see people and objects located miles away and behind walls. I do not possess this ability. In fact, many women have told me this gift has been given to women, not men. However, I know for a fact that some men can telecast see, but they are few and far between. Some have told me that one's aura enables telecast seeing, while others have said it involves using presence. I believe that telecast seeing is done through the eyes, that by sensing the images that go to a person's brain, telecasters can then see them for themselves. This belief has been confirmed thousands of times. Telecast seeing seems to involve reading the brain instead of sensing the eyes, but I know I must be looking at something for someone to telecast see through me. If my eyes are closed, the telecaster cannot see either.

Telecast seeing is a challenge because people keep its techniques a secret. I am always told that telecast seeing is not for spying on women or other inappropriate actions, even though I have no such intentions. I want to use telecast seeing for the same reasons it has become so popular, namely helping others and expanding my mind. In addition, without telecast seeing, one cannot telecast long distances. Yet, every time I inquire about its use, I am sent on a wild goose chase. While trying to telecast see, I have noticed people mimicking various scenarios to trick me and convince me that I am seeing something that isn't real. This is very frustrating, but I will keep trying until I master this skill. I suspect this ability is open to moral minds that communicate on much higher frequencies. Once a person is above the frequency that sabotage is possible, it may open. There are two frequencies that people move past—the evil line and the sabotage line. The evil line is the frequency that all evil can hear. The sabotage line is higher, but I think all frequencies higher than that are from moral people only. Great intellect and abilities open past the sabotage line.

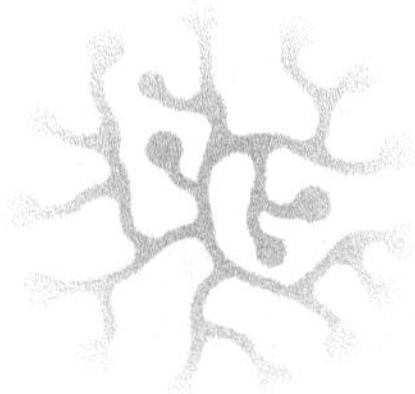

Auras

THE AURA HAS BEEN MISREPRESENTED by hundreds of television shows and spiritual books. These sources depict it as a halo over a person's head or an energy form surrounding objects and people. The aura may turn different colours depending on a person's emotions, and each object may represent different colours using the aura's energy radiance. While these things are true, whatever this coloured halo or energy is, it is not an aura and must be given a different name.

Auras are electronic visual representations of whatever your mind wants to make. A true aura is a replication of an object, person, or animal. A person can replicate anything in size, colour, or shape using the aura. The aura is much more transparent than real objects, making it easy to identify. A person can place an aura anywhere within another person's range. I have not been able to determine how far the aura can go since I can only visualize it as far as the horizon. In addition, even though I perceive the aura on the horizon, it could be located anywhere between the horizon and myself. It is even possible that the aura falls within my eight-car radius, but I believe it can travel further.

The process of manifesting an aura is difficult to explain. When I first started playing with the aura, I found it extremely difficult to control. The process was explained to me as simply imagining an object in front of you and then attempting to move it around. I then experimented with colours and shapes, always keeping in mind that an aura can mask another aura. In other words, if you are unsuccessful in your first attempt at moving an aura, this may mean that the aura is masked by another aura.

Many people use auras, so unless you see an aura first, it may be difficult to duplicate it because you don't know its original form. One technique to determine what an aura looks like is to point your index fingers at each other and make them touch. Stare at them until you see a floating finger in the middle. Then, pull your fingers apart slightly, and you will notice that one finger is more transparent than the other. While you are not seeing the aura, you are experiencing an optical illusion that adequately represents what an aura looks like. Once you get the concept, spotting auras becomes easy.

It is possible to diminish someone else's aura projection. You can mask it by creating a black area or a transparent field on the projected aura. You can also make a person's projected aura more vibrant, noticeable, and colourful by duplicating it in the same spot.

An amazing thing about auras is that you can see them when they are projected beside or behind you and don't need your eyes to see them. I like to project auras in front of me to see them with my eyes. In fact, I am not seeing them with my eyes, but I am seeing where to place them in relation to other objects. While auras can pass through objects and barriers such as windows, when driving, I like to keep them in front of the car, where I can see them in relation to the car. To create an aura behind me, I use the rear-view mirror to place it. Since I cannot telecast see, this is the only way I can do it. I am perfectly capable of projecting auras behind me, but in the interest of placement, I like seeing them.

As a Telepathic Icon, I have been able to take the aura to another level, an aura musical show. Since I telepathize everything I hear, I use auras to create a rock band. For example, when driving, I project auras onto oncoming traffic and play with music and lights. I am musically inclined, so in my mind, I strum the guitar and play the drums as if I would in a real band. At this point, I find it difficult to play more than two instruments at a time. I keep attempting to play the entire band and multi-coloured lights, but I think I have reached my plateau. Sometimes I am fortunate to be surrounded by people who join me in my music-making. I particularly enjoy this activity because I can defy the laws of gravity and play upside down.

I like to change my performances to reflect the season. For example, I create goblins, pumpkins, ghosts, witches, and other Halloween characters on Halloween. For Christmas, I play Christmas songs using the aura of Santa in his sleigh, snowflakes, presents, and Christmas trees. I use elves to clean people's cars and place mistletoe over woman's heads before giving them a friendly kiss. On Valentine's Day, I play romantic music and turn auras into cupids that shoot people with love arrows and make aura hearts come out of their chests.

Telepathizing everything I hear causes me to have more telepathic conversations with people than the average person. As a truck driver, I can communicate daily with thousands of people. When I drive down a road, I hear everything going on around me. Sometimes I receive aura kisses from the ladies, and other times I get complaints about how loud I am playing my music. While most of the comments are positive, I find it hardest to satisfy everybody's taste in music. For the people in the oncoming traffic, it's not much of an issue since I'm only within their range for a few seconds. People in front, beside, and behind me usually argue about the music. While I try to please everyone by playing various music, I like blue-collar music. Country music is a bit too slow, so I listen to fast songs with good guitar riffs instead. The elderly don't like my music and call it a racket, but I don't worry about it because I don't encounter too many of them on the road.

I have noticed that high school students complain that I'm not playing music that is "cool." In the future, I could buy the latest CDs, pop them into the CD player and imitate the artists with the aura. It's hard to please everyone because some teenagers are into R&B, and others are into rap music or rock. I am willing to try, though, and perhaps alternate music on different days of the week. Elementary and junior high kids don't seem as fussy, so I can play anything for them and please them. I typically direct all my attention to children when they are around, regardless of their age. This is because kids are just awakening to their telepathic consciousness, and I offer myself to them as a learning aid. Some parents have told me not to bother and that they will teach their kids telepathy themselves. However, I believe no man is an island, and it takes a community to raise a child. When I tell this to parents, most use me as an aid and welcome my interaction with their kids. I also direct my attention to tourists since they are usually curious about what I sound like and what my aura shows look like.

Numerous health professionals (doctors, psychiatrists, paramedics, nurses) have telecasted on me and told me that telepathy and auras are only for communication, not entertainment. Some have even called me an anarchist. While I can't stop telepathizing everything I hear, extensive use of the aura for entertainment and educational reasons is my choice. Some of my critics are very aggressive, so to get them off my back, I agree with them, and once they are gone, I continue with whatever I am doing. While using auras for communication only may be the norm, I am the only person with the gift to entertain using my aura. I have been taught to use my gifts, and I intend to continue doing so in the future.

I am a truck driver by profession and spend a lot of time on the road. Therefore, I can educate the masses about the sixth sense by bending the rules. I can also entertain people with a good grasp of the sixth sense. Negative side effects of my telepathy include annoying people who don't like the music I am playing. Some said I am also responsible for sending people into the psych ward. I am not bothered by this because being committed is not life-threatening, with most people released in about a month. Secondly, a group of people having the same delusion at the same time substantiates the sixth sense. While my truck music playing and sending out auras is evidence, doctors do not like publicizing the fact, even though they don't disprove my actions. Once I plant the seed, it's not my responsibility to coach others through the awakening process to its conclusion. My role is to provide evidence, and society dictates the rest. Thirdly, while I may have put people in the psych ward and on medication, I also planted in them a seed that acknowledges the existence of the sixth sense. Since nobody else could reach them, I did them a favour.

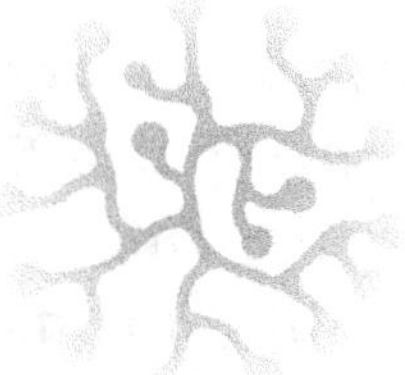

Tracing

IT WAS DIFFICULT FOR ME to learn tracing. I approached it scientifically and devised many theories and tests before I figured it out. Tracing is simply feeling the spot from which a voice is emanating. We can pinpoint the source of a sound with our ears, and telepathy uses the same concept to pinpoint telepathic transmissions. I can feel the source of the transmission, but I cannot judge the distance. Therefore, while I may know that the voice is coming from the northwest, I don't know how far away its origin is located. In addition, while it is easy to know where an aura is, knowing where it emanates from is almost impossible without systematically reading the minds of the people around you.

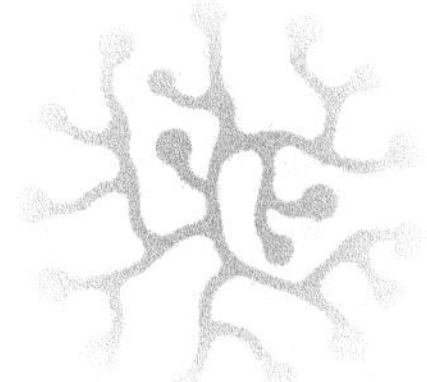

Transferring Smells and Tastes

IT IS POSSIBLE TO TRANSFER smell and taste onto a person, but I rarely exercise this skill because I fear this may make a person delusional since they might not have enough knowledge of telepathy to deal with the experience properly. However, I welcome the smell and taste transfers onto me. These transfers come in waves and don't happen very often. To transfer smell and taste, you must imagine a taste or smell and transfer that image onto someone else. The transfers aren't as powerful as real smells or tastes, but you can tell what is being depicted. Fortunately, almost all the sixth sense smells I have encountered have been pleasant, except for one instance when someone synthesized urine and kept telling me I had hepatitis. Such pranks are unavoidable, but I wish people didn't toy with other people's feelings in such an insensitive manner.

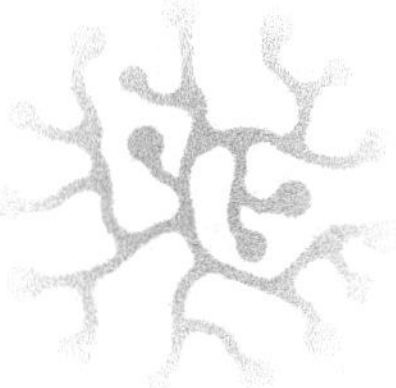

Dream Casting

IT IS POSSIBLE TO ALTER the course of someone's dream or cast a dream onto a sleeping person. I have had many dreams in which I had woken up my neighbour and asked him whether he liked his dream. The neighbour would tell me parts of the dream and point out the parts he made up. I cannot telecast without eye vision, so I have not done this myself. However, it has been done to me thousands of times. Though we can generate dreams on our own, I would say that many of our early morning dreams are telepathically generated since people may be awake to change our dreams. At the very least, this is true in my case.

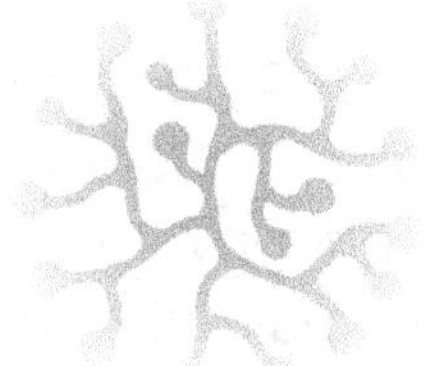

Sensing the Future

I USED TO BELIEVE THAT the ability to predict the future resulted from trickery. I have had many experiences where I thought I had read the future, but I later found that my experience was nothing more than telepathic communication with a group of people who carry out a pre-determined future.

Later in life, I encountered people who could really see the past and future. Sometimes timelines change in the future, and they were always aware of them. Down-low speaking, I cannot see timelines or the past. Many people communicate with others by showing memories. I do not communicate this way very often. But it is the norm for most people.

Some might argue that when people become aware that their loved one, located miles away, had been in a car accident or passed away, this represents forecasting the future. However, these may also be simple examples of telecasting: people are around the victim, or sometimes the victims telecast on their loved ones and tell them what happened prior to physical proof. Sometimes we find out things that happened telepathically before we get physical proof. This isn't sensing the future, but it happens all the time.

Timelines are something people can see. Some people can see the past and future well. With enough actions, timelines change. Timelines are not all set in stone. Also, there are ways of obscuring the past and timelines through electrical signal attacks, otherwise known as nic nacs. Criminals do this a lot, where they cover up their crimes to hide them. The obscured timeline or memory becomes apparent by making a telepathic link with shrouds, nic nacs, obscured future, and past timelines, with a heat source such as a fire. Heat sources like the sun often eventually take off nic nacs, shrouds, etc. Sometimes they can be washed off. In a world of organized crime by the Illuminati, timelines and memories were often hidden, and it was a fight to make the truth known.

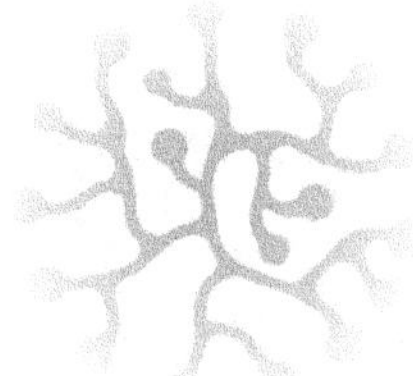

Nic Nacs

SOME PEOPLE CALL NIC NACS the spice of life. There are good and bad nic nacs. Many people put electrical signals in or on objects like auras on an object. I don't personally see them, but I always hear about them. However, because I always tell the truth, people nic nac me a lot. People use nic nacs to discover things. If a nic nac sticks, it's usually true. People don't realize that when a group of clones vectored in the zillions nic nac something and maintain it, it looks like fact when it isn't. When nic nacs are exposed to conscience, the sun or a fire heat source such as energized electron heat, the nic nacs usually dissipate unless they are true. Electron heat or energized electrons make bad or false nic nacs go away.

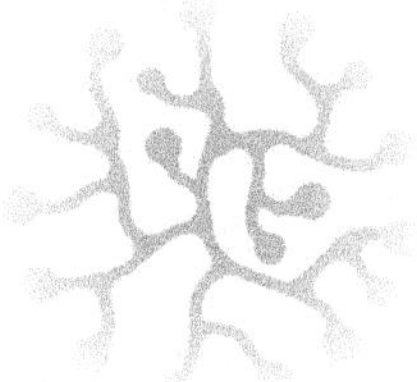

Telekinesis

TELEKINESIS IS WHEN OTHERS CONTROL people through their minds. I have observed that when a telecasting person emits an electrical signal more powerful than an electrical signal my body emits, they can control my physical body. It happens to everyone. Telekinesis can happen by sending foreign electrical signals through nerves of the body, including the brain and influencing electrons to move in a direction and moving molecules or objects. So there are two different kinds of telekinesis.

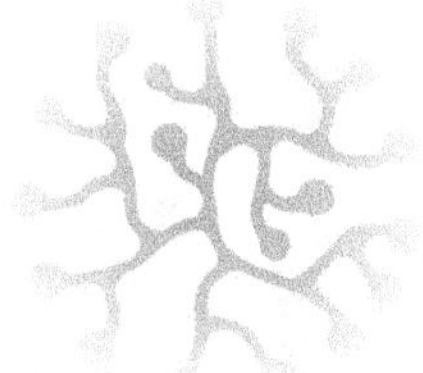

Telepathy with Animals

EVEN THOUGH I HAVE NEVER communicated with animals using telepathy for most of my life, I have observed others doing it. At first, I suspected I was made fun of, but it is equally possible I was being closed-minded. Human and animal brains aren't that different. However, animals do not understand language in the way humans do. Therefore, while humans can telepathically communicate with each other in complete sentences the same way they talk, animals are incapable of returning or even understanding such communication. This is like an animal only understanding commands. I believe animals can see auras and can experience the full range of telepathy that people can. I suppose that with repetition and rewards, an animal can be taught to respond to telepathic commands. I also suspect that dogs would be more receptive to telepathy than cats because they have higher intelligence. Getting an animal to obey a telepathic command may require painstaking effort. Personally, I am not as interested in attempting to establish telepathic connections with animals as with humans. Moreover, efforts to establish telepathic links with animals can easily be interrupted and mimicked by other people and can cause problems with your efforts. Later in life, my cat Mocha communicated with me from time to time. A cat's language is different from a human's, but they understand emotions. She said she loved me. As time went by, I discovered that many animals, trees, rocks, etc., are telepathic, but because of telepathic crime threats, they rarely show themselves where evil can hear them. They seem to only communicate with those they trust and when the situation is safe. Then they go back to hiding.

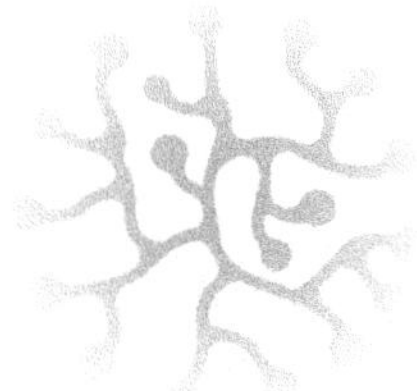

Telepathizing All and the Fame That Followed

WHEN I WAS SEVEN, MY grandfather asked me what I wanted to do with my life. I replied that I wanted to be a doctor or a lawyer. Hearing this, he told me, "No, grandson. You want to be a forest ranger and live on acreage since you love the environment so much." I bought into this and followed it for many years. I even enrolled in Forest Management Studies at the University of Alberta. However, in my twenties, I realized something was wrong. I quit my studies, and when, a year later, I became telepathically conscious, I finally understood why. My grandfather was trying to keep me from people because of my socially awkward gift. He meant well, but it wasn't the best thing for me or others. People need proof of telepathy regularly, and I can provide it. My gift should be used in populated areas, not hidden away in the bush.

I don't know how long I've been famous, whether the media publicized me when I was a child or whether I became famous when awakening to telepathy. The name "Telepathic Icon" is not something I made up; it is what others have called me for as long as I've been telepathic.

I don't know whether media coverage about me is contained in North America or worldwide. All I know is that when I meet tourists from Canada and the United States, they seem to know who I am. I meet 99% of the tourists when I'm on the road. It's not hard to tell the tourists apart from the locals by looking at the license plate. Moreover, I always listen to music when I drive to make myself identifiable to people, share my gift with them and help wake people up to telepathy. Since I can trace, I also know where the tourists' voices are coming from when they establish communication with me. I usually shake aura hands with the men and kiss the ladies' hands with my aura. They usually ask, "Barry? Is it you?"

I confirm my identity and reassure them that I telepathize everything I hear while listening to the radio. Usually, the tourists I meet invite me to visit their city or country.

One aspect of my telepathic ability that I don't quite understand is my ability to communicate with live media. This is the only type of media with which I can communicate. I have tried to telepathize pre-recorded shows and sitcoms but without success. On the other hand, while I can telepathize everything, I only hear within an eight-car radius; distance doesn't seem to be a factor in my communication with the media. I talk to the media in the United States and Canada all the time. I don't have a satellite dish, so I haven't been able to test how well-known I am around the globe by watching broadcasts from all over the world. However, a media personality from Sydney, Australia, knew who I was, and I communicated with people from Russia and Baghdad through television. I have not yet found a station that didn't know who I was, and as soon as I tune in, someone begins communicating with me. I am unsure who is telecasting during these communications—my conversation partner or me. I cannot see the people I'm talking to, so they must be telecast seeing, not me. I might also be simply hearing them through the television set. At the same time, I am positive that the television is not their means of hearing long distances and that they are telecasting.

While I am sure that this mode of communication is only for the famous, it is unclear from my perspective whether other people are covered in telepathic media. While I am sure there is only one Telepathic Icon (me), it makes sense that another one could exist. I don't go out of my way to contact the media. Sometimes, I have been contacted by the media following a live broadcast. This usually happens when I listen to a radio station for a long time. The media will often eavesdrop on me between broadcasts and reports on what I have been doing. Some might call this an invasion of privacy, but I don't mind if I'm not doing something private. If anybody could get in contact with the media, chaos would result. Therefore, it seems that for communication to be established, both people must be willing to create a connection. When communicating with the media, I don't go out of my way to catch attention. I simply say something back, and I am always heard. I have also discovered that on many occasions, my neighbour played a prank on me by talking over the television set. My neighbour's imitation of the newscaster was awful, and the content of her "broadcast" was completely inconsistent with what a media person might say. These instances were short-term, and no harm came of them except for my inability to hear what the media was communicating.

I greatly enjoy using my telepathic ability to entertain the telepathic population. However, the most satisfying aspect of my telepathic communication is awakening a child. Dozens of parents and kids have thanked me for helping them discover the magic of telepathy. I must have woken hundreds of others, which also gives me great joy.

While telepathizing everything I hear has given me an interesting public and professional life, my private life isn't as great. I tend to move around often because I wear out my neighbours' patience. In some places, I have been banned from watching television, listening to the radio, and taking long showers because I would turn everything I heard into telepathy and the neighbours would hear. Whenever I move to a new house, my neighbours think my gift is cool and are glad to have a celebrity nearby at first, but after a while, they find the sounds constantly emanating from my house annoying and try to block them. I have been made to wear earplugs in the past to drown out what I hear and stop myself from turning it into telepathy, but they don't work very well. I try to read a lot and keep quiet to keep the peace. I live where they've accepted my gift and don't treat it as a nuisance. I am now able to watch television again. I try to keep the volume down, and since the houses are spaced further apart, the neighbours are not as sensitive to the noise I generate. Whatever the reason, I find the neighbourhood a wonderful place to live and telepathize. Years ago, I learned how to shut off telepathizing everything I hear and how to turn it on. I learned to think about sound and then project it. When I didn't want to telepathize everything I heard, I simply didn't think of the sound for projection anymore. I learned to control it.

Before I was telepathically conscious, I moved around a lot because I wanted to travel. For example, I moved all over Alberta. In Calgary, I learned about telepathy, was trained to be a celebrity, and received the call to move to Vancouver. This is because after living in Calgary for three years and becoming fully functional from the telepathic perspective, it was time to move to a bigger city and reach a larger audience. Thus, my desire to educate others about telepathy is now driving my travels. I am unsure how long I will remain in Vancouver, and while my truck driving allows me to reach a wide audience, I'd like to make the whole world know about telepathy someday and may do things differently.

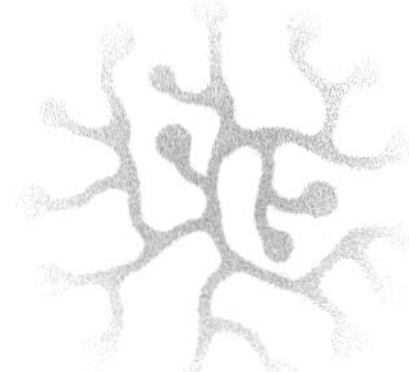

The Sixth Sense and the Education System

SADLY, ALTHOUGH MOST OF THE population can be telepathic and telepathy is an accepted form of communication, it is not part of the education system. However, things might change in the future. In the 1980s, when I attended school, I was taught about the five senses: taste, smell, touch, sight, and hearing. When I was a senior, a teacher pulled me aside in the hallway and showed me a new textbook, acknowledging the sixth sense. The book didn't go into much detail about the sixth sense, but it was a start. I know the teacher wanted to show me the new textbook because she knew I was unconscious of telepathy at the time. I thank her for trying. If I had my way, my child and all children would learn about telepathy as a part of the curriculum.

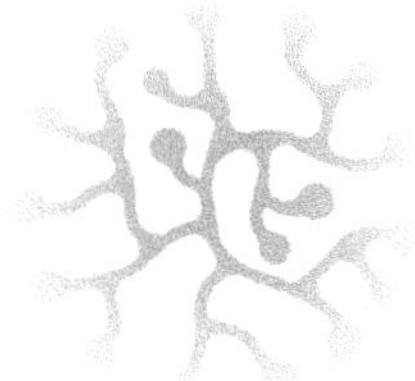

Telepathic Brainwashing

THIS MIGHT SEEM FAR-FETCHED, BUT I have observed that telepathically advanced people, such as businessmen and members of the upper class, work together as a team. Since I telepathize everything I hear and the media widely cover me, I stick out like a sore thumb and am not difficult to locate. Therefore, inflicting a group punishment on me through telecasting isn't difficult.

Now that I am completely aware of telepathy, it is much harder to be convinced telepathically to commit a crime. While I am not a criminal at heart and wouldn't engage in criminal activity on my own accord, I acknowledge that some people have attempted to persuade me telepathically to do so. Looking back on my past, I recall being often bombarded with thoughts telling me to do bad things. It happens to everyone from time to time. These thoughts weren't my own; I was being telepathically brainwashed. Now that I am aware of telepathic brainwashing, I can fight it off. I make a consistent effort to do so because I want to travel the world and need to keep and maintain a clean criminal record. But I must say for people who aren't telepathic, mind control can make people do things they wouldn't normally do.

Organized crime Illuminati often try to telepathically convince others to commit crimes or do something evil. This compresses the person's electrical field, leaving them permanently without knowledge. Then they become a slave or oppressed person indefinitely, doing small menial jobs and never gaining intellect. Thus, they are easy to control through mind control.

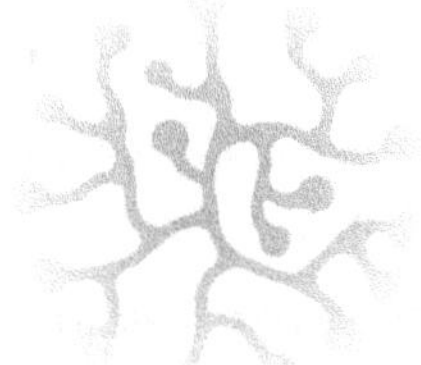

The Sixth Sense and Psychiatry

SEVERAL MENTAL ILLNESSES LIST HEARING voices as their symptom. In many cases, however, the supposed mentally ill are hearing other peoples' thoughts. This is not an illness but a form of communication. The psychiatric field won't acknowledge telepathy because there is no way to measure it. Scientific devices that measure telepathic brain waves or other ways of measurable transmission have been developed but not applied to psychiatry, and without scientific measurement, psychiatrists are free to use their judgment to determine who is affected by mental illness. The trap of thinking that a belief in telepathy makes you mentally ill is dangerous, so very few venture down the path of open discussion. Moreover, psychiatrists treat everything with medication, remedying the symptoms but not addressing the source of the problem. Thus, the psychiatric field aims to blame the victim rather than telepathic violence. In many instances, people become telepathic predators, inflicting delusional thoughts on others. These predators may keep the victims awake at night and drive them crazy. This is not as difficult to accomplish as one might think, as persistent suggestions can make people do things they wouldn't do otherwise. Thus, telepathic brainwashing may land a person in the psych ward regardless of medication.

Schizophrenia lists hallucinations and delusions as its symptoms. Those affected by this disease are victims of telepathic brainwashing, which causes their delusions. Hallucinations and hearing and seeing things that are not there are merely the person hearing telepathy and seeing the aura. Some have made this connection, and others have not. I have observed that schizophrenics don't follow the rules. They talk to the voices in their head with their verbal, making schizophrenics appear odd to people around them. Schizophrenics may chase auras around in anger and frustration instead of simply ignoring or using them to communicate with others. A rule society seems to follow is don't mix the sixth sense with the physical. Answer telepathy with telepathy and answer verbal with verbal. Never mix telepathy with verbal. It's a habit, and people can be trained to look less odd. They may not have the telepathic education to understand what they are sensing; they may also be confused or unable to distinguish between sounds inside their head and those communicated to them orally; it is also possible that they may have annoying telepathic habits that cause them to be preyed upon by other people.

Bipolar psychosis affects people in other ways. Patients tend to avoid mixing the sixth and fifth senses and don't face the same awkward problems as schizophrenics. Instead, they are preyed upon by other people, fed delusional thoughts, and kept awake for nights at a time. This brainwashing makes bipolar patients do things they wouldn't normally do. The one-time victims of this so-called illness may be victims of random acts of telepathic violence or losers in a telepathic fight gone wrong. Those for whom bipolar disorder causes frequent problems may be victims of a telepathic serial predator or be preyed upon for bad telepathic habits.

Reasons for nervous breakdowns are wide and varied. Since no laws protect people against telepathic predation, people may enjoy and get away with a lifetime of telepathic crime. In addition to a misdemeanour, some people might get into telepathic feuds with others and drive each other crazy. I telepathize everything I hear, so when I watch television or listen to the radio, I used to annoy my neighbours with the non-stop telepathic sounds coming from the house. This may cause feuds or lead to predation on the part of the neighbours. Doctors often prescribe pills that help people sleep or stabilize emotions in the event of predatory delusions. However, these pills may negatively affect one's health and shorten one's lifespan. In addition, the pills may help the victim cope for a short while, but the mental imbalance caused by stress, lack of sleep, and anxiety will surely return once the victim returns home and telecasting predation resumes. Hence, the victims usually end up in the hospital repeatedly, and pills become their mainstay.

Psychiatry usually only focuses on the physical, chemical, and psychological aspects of mental illness. The one thing they need to do is acknowledge the truth of the electronic. Negative charged electrons or souls is an electrical sickness and is treated by the teachings from high energy electron sources. However, there are also telepathic crime victims, and this is a form of electrical signal attack. Telepathic crime victims need to be placed in an anti-telepathic room to shield them from telepathic attacks. If the telepathic recording device was invented, we could place it around the person's neck and conduct tests of the telepathic signals the telepathic crime victim receives. Neural interfaces have been invented, so recording an electrical signal isn't difficult. We can even detect electronic murder signatures if we want to. If we found, measured, and recorded the telepathic attacks coming from another person, we could treat it as a telepathic crime. We could relay the identity to the police. If the police couldn't deal with it, they would relay it to the military. If the military couldn't deal with it, they would relay the threat to the vectored military individual.

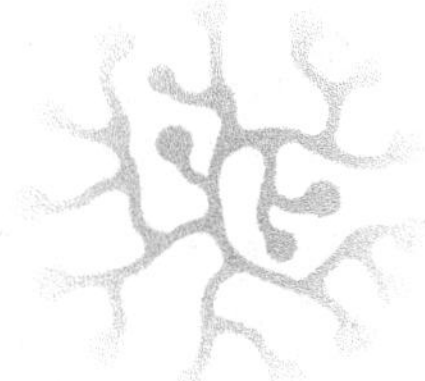

Anti-Telepathic Houses

I STRUGGLED TO FIND OUT what anti-telepathic substances were for a long time. It took me years to figure it out. I went on quite a journey.

Most telepaths get along with their neighbours or avoid them entirely. However, for some of the population, this isn't the case. For these people, anti-telepathic houses should become mandatory, and they may become the norm once the general population accepts telepathy as a legitimate mode of communication. While I have not generated enough funds to test anti-telepathic houses, I hope to do so in the future. The test will involve erecting an airtight box, playing offensive music inside, and waiting for the neighbours' reactions. I will test boxes made of wood, drywall, glass, and, most importantly, stone. I predict that stone will be the best material for an anti-telepathic house. While driving, I noticed that I could not penetrate concrete tunnel walls. I could communicate with the cars on my side of the tunnel but could not reach those beyond it.

People have indicated to me that I transmit louder in the rain or intense fog. I tend to get these reports after I've been in one place for a while. These people have a point of reference and have heard me numerous times. However, I do not know if this is true since I haven't conducted scientific tests to prove it.

I also found that the worst telepathic inhibitor is glass. As I walk through the house, telepathic transmissions increase in frequency and volume beside windows. Since the building code mandates that every house have at least one window, using glass cannot be avoided. In addition, a house made entirely of concrete, with only a few windows, would be dim, illuminated only by artificial light. Secondly, you would create a condensation trap, with moisture having nowhere to escape. Such a house would never pass a health inspection and would, in fact, be extremely uncomfortable.

I found rock glass to be a solution for the moisture and window problem. To produce rock glass, you would need a clear stone like obsidian. It could be melted down and shaped into panes of desired thickness. These rock windows wouldn't be as transparent as glass but would do a good job of letting in light. Since an anti-telepathic house requires thick walls, the difference between the thickness of walls and windows will be unusual and may require extremely thick windows. In my case, I only need thick walls around important rooms—my bedroom and TV room. Thus, I could use concrete drywall to fortify the exterior and interior walls of the bedroom and TV room. Concrete roof tiles would also be used, but this isn't the perfect solution because of ventilation demands. I would also have to specialize the doors leading into these rooms. Building such a specialized house requires a lot of funds, and I must postpone experiments until I can afford it.

The ramification of living in an anti-telepathic house endangers one's peaceful, quiet, and private life. For me, an anti-telepathic house would allow me to raise my kids. Children are too noisy for my gift, and I would continuously test my neighbours' patience. Since neither of these is viable, I will spend the rest of my days trying to make enough money to build an anti-telepathic house.

My needs for an anti-telepathic house may differ from others in that I don't want to cause problems for my neighbours, but everyone needs anti-telepathic walls occasionally. I need them to shield me from telepathic attacks. All people receive telepathic attacks. When people are too bombarded, they may need an anti-telepathic roomed psychiatry ward to shield them from the attacks until the police or military deal with the telepathic crime problem. Also, we need anti-telepathic courtrooms so that judges, witnesses, lawyers, or the jury are not subjected to telepathic attacks or death threats.

Years ago, I discovered that plastic is an anti-telepathic substance. As mentioned previously, we use plastic to shield wires from electricity or electrical signals from leaving the wire. Therefore, plastic would work for an anti-telepathic wall. If we need windows, we can use clear plastic. A six-sided walled room made of plastic would be anti-telepathic. I made the discovery years back, about the year 2016.

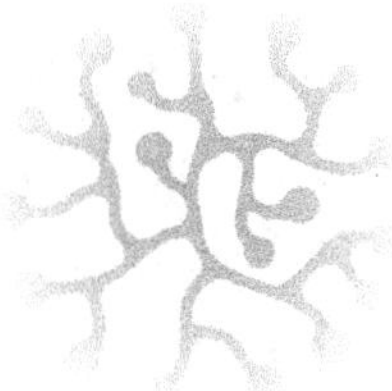

Conclusions

IT IS STRANGE THAT TELEPATHY is so widespread yet so rarely talked about; that most of the population believes in its existence, yet it is not taught in the school curriculum; that mental illnesses such as schizophrenia, bipolar disorder, and psychosis are so improperly treated; that anti-telepathic houses are not common; and that I am famous but have never signed an autograph. The threat of telepathic criminals is vast and real. It is the norm to only talk about the sixth sense in the sixth sense. Of course, few people have seen my name in print or heard it said on the evening news. However, this is going to change. I believe we must change our views on telepathy. There is nothing wrong, creepy, or weird about telepathy. It is a form of communication and should be embraced like all the other senses. The fact that a Telepathic Icon (me) exists proves we are moving towards accepting telepathy, not banishing it.

I hope this book will increase awareness of telepathy as a legitimate communication form. I intended to cut out the nonsense and deliver the facts. It took me many years to gather all the facts in this book. I was the subject of many pranks and jokes, but mine doesn't have to be the path of every unconscious telepathic person. I realize that my account of telecasting is incomplete, but it is a step in the right direction; sometimes, we need to acknowledge that something exists before it is fully understood.

Many in the psychiatric field will undoubtedly object to my views based on their beliefs that a chemical imbalance causes voices in one's head. They are partly right because delusions are worsened by stress, lack of sleep, and food deprivation. All I ask is that psychiatric professionals open their minds to the sixth sense, even if it cannot yet be measured. The patient's delusions may not accurately represent what is real, but their source is a telepathic criminal, not the victim. I sincerely hope psychiatry acknowledges that the electronic is just as important as the chemical and biological in mental illness diagnosis and treatment.

Since I telepathize everything I hear, I hope to build a house that is anti-telepathic. In doing so, I will be able to make as much noise as I want without disturbing my neighbours. I also hope to tour the world and meet the many earthlings who possess the gift of telepathy. I have set up a website at www.barryaubinauthor.com, where anybody can contact me through email. Depending on the volume of the emails I receive, I will attempt to answer as many people as possible.

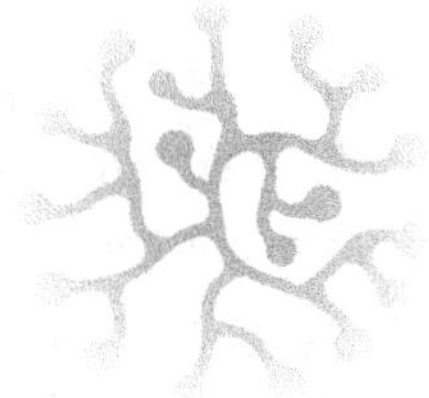

References

N.C.Durham New York times New York June 22 1971 Page 22

Dean Radin The Conscious Universe New York HarperCollins Publishers Inc 1997 Page 31

Daniel Boy The French and Parascience Twenty years of Surveys Revue Francaise De Sociologie 2004 2005 Volume 45 Page 49-59

Anthony Cuthbertson Brain computer interfaces will make people telepathic, scientists say independent.co.uk September 10 2019

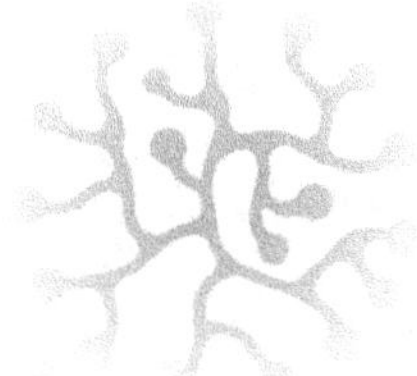

About the Author

It was the year 1999 and Barry was driving around doing a night job as a truck driver. He had been perplexed with the world problems for some time. Searching for answers, Eureka! Barry had a major epiphany moment. Barry found out telepathy existed, that he was world famous, and that the world was in a serious state of environmental disrepair. The top 20 scientists of the world issued a warning to humanity that unless humanity acted fast, the world would reach a tipping point very soon where all life may perish. At that point, Barry turned telepathy and fixing the world his life. Born a deep thinker, Barry works to solve the worlds greatest problems by getting to the root of things. How deep the rabbit hole goes surprised Barry, but no task is insurmountable. We can do this.

www.ingramcontent.com/pod-product-compliance
Lightning Source LLC
Chambersburg PA
CBHW080503030726
47592CB00011B/3235